Survival Cooking:
25 Simple and Nutritious Recipes to Cook in The Wilderness

Table of Contents

Introduction

I would like to thank and congratulate you on downloading *"Survival: 25 Simple and Nutritious Food Recipes to Cook Using Your Emergency Supplies!"* With the world in turmoil and with natural and man-made disasters on the rise it is best to prepare yourself for the worst.

An important part of this preparation is gathering a food supply that can help you to survive through an emergency situation should you find yourself in one. You will certainly feel much more at ease in knowing that you have stored food and water supplies in your pantry that will keep you and your loved ones from starving. You want to try and store away as much food for an emergency that you can, as you do not know how long the emergency situation could last.

Preparing yourself for those times in life that are not planned or expected can make the ordeal much easier for you if you are well-stocked up on emergency supplies.

Being prepared is half the battle in these emergency situations, it will certainly make it much easier for you and your loved ones to cope with if you are stocked up on food and water. I hope that you will find my suggestions and recipes beneficial to you in preparing yourself for an emergency situation.

Chapter 1. Basic Survival Techniques

People that plan for emergency situations are often referred to as preppers or survivalists. They gather and store supplies that they believe they will need if they find themselves in an emergency situation.

These actions that they take are those of people who want to survive and thrive even through an emergency situation. The actions of preppers are those of survival. There are so many different things that could happen in life that could have deep effects on us, making sure that we are prepared for the worse is going to make it that much easier to survive those tough times.

First Step

Once you have decided that you want to start prepping and gathering emergency supplies you may even want to consider joining a prepper community. You can join a prepper community either through the internet or in real life.

Preppers are known to be shy by nature. It could take you some time before you will meet with them face to face, as they do not like to reveal that they have supplies of food, water, shelter etc.

Many view prepping as a kind of insurance policy for an unseen future. A person can choose to spend a large amount of money to build their emergency supplies up or a limited amount. When it comes to prepping there is no right or wrong way as long as your prepping will suit your personal needs in an emergency situation.

Be Innovative

It is very important to be innovative and a quick thinker, be prepared to tackle whatever life may throw at you. In your preparedness you should include cover maximum expected points you may face in the future while also keeping in mind things you have faced in the past.

For example if you live in an area where you have experienced in the past many power failures during heavy snowfalls and land sliding cutting off power lines then you might want to think of ways you can survive without electricity. Prepare yourself to live without electricity for an extended period of time.

Having the security of food supplies for an emergency situation will be one of the most important steps in preparing yourself and loved ones for an emergency situation.

This is why growing your own food source is a great idea as well as making as many food items from scratch as you can. You may find that you cannot get access to local grocery stores during an emergency so having your own garden will help keep you in fresh foods.

Things such as a land slide could prevent traffic from getting to your area so there is no way the transport trucks that deliver the food supplies to local stores can get through. If gas prices go to high the truckers could go on strike and you could be out of a food supply from that.

There is many things in life that we are not prepared for, but you can make some emergency preparations that can make these hard times easier. Having an emergency supply of food and water is certainly a good start as a prepper.

Know What You Are Preparing For

In our world today disasters are happening at an alarming rate anytime and anywhere. You need to be aware of the facts and figures of the area where you are living. Know what kind of disaster is most likely to occur in your area. This knowledge can help you to plan more thoroughly and precisely for a disaster.

When you are deciding what kind of disaster to plan for it will also determine the type of survival technique that you will need to follow. If for example you reside in an area that is well-known for earthquakes and flooding, the items you choose will be different from survival items chosen in a war or attach situation.

The best way for you to plan is to prepare yourself for the worst case scenario. Being completely prepared is the reasoning behind preppers. For many planners it is basically a state of mind.

Types of Preppers

There is many different types of preppers. There are short and long term preppers. The short term preppers are looking to cover a time period from a few days to a couple of months. It is a good idea that all families have at least a short term food supply in stock in case of unforeseen storms that prevents them from getting food supplies in for example.

The long term preppers generally do planning for disasters that will leave a long term effect, so they plan for longer self-sufficiency in the event that a disaster may occur.

Food Storage Tips

Learning about food storage tips is important so that you can make your food last longer during an emergency situation. Proper storing techniques will help to save your health during a time of crisis.

You will be able to keep almost every kind of food in your pantry. You will be able to add a variety of food to your pantry using proper storing techniques. One of the best options for storing foods is canned foods. Plan to collect items that will quickly vanish in an emergency situation.

Purified Water and Seltzer Water

Water should be the number one item on your list because without it we will not survive. Distilled water is the purest form of water. Start collecting water now and plan to get more water. Also add canned seltzer water to your pantry, canned seltzer will last indefinitely. It is a great addition to your water supply and will also help with constipation. If you have acidity avoid seltzer.

Add canned liquids

Canned foods with high liquid content are important to add to food store. Two great examples are vegetable juice and pineapple juice. They will provide nutrition and hydration. Canned coconut milk and evaporated milk are also good to add to supplies.

You can use coconut milk to help cook your rice faster. Dried tomatoes, meat stock, and vegetables can help to cook your rice without using your drinking water.

Cheeses encased in Wax

Hard waxed cheeses are very hard to find, but they are available. Swiss, Parmesan and sharp cheddar or Gouda encased in wax is difficult to find. The wax helps prevent the cheese from becoming infected with mold or bacteria while keeping the cheese moisturized, so it can be stored for a very long time without being refrigerated.

Parmesan is a heavy cheese, it can survive for more than three months in it powdered form. When it is encased in wax it can last for up to 25 years! The wax will keep hard cheeses moist.

Tang, Coffee, Tea and Ovaltine

The coffee will help to increase mental alertness which will be very useful during a survival situation. The tea is good to help with mental relaxation. You can quickly hydrate with tea. Tang is known as a prepper classic to add flavor to water supply.

Bouillon cubes will be useful they are basically compressed stock. They will help to add salty flavor to your soups and gravies. You may want to keep them in your preppers pantry even if you do not use them as they could come in handy as something to barter with.

Other survival foods items are:

* canned and dehydrated poultry, meats and seafood

* oils, lard, butter, organic shortening, olive oil etc.

* Whole wheat flour

* potato flour

- baking soda and baking powder

- nuts, seeds, and nut butters

- beans and legumes

- canned fruit and veggies

- jams and jellies

- raisins, dried fruits and fruit strips

- potato flakes and gratin potatoes

- crackers

- shelf stable ready to eat meals

- bread crumbs and stuffing

Chapter 2. Dehydrator Meals

In this chapter I will share some dehydrator recipes with you that I am sure you will find will come in handy during an emergency situation but you can also cook these meals in an oven.

But for this chapter we will focus on making them using a dehydrator. You will have four dehydrator recipes in this chapter that will come in handy to know as a prepper.

Meat Dehydrator Recipes

Ground Beef

Dehydrating ground beef

- First you want to select extra-lean ground beef, bison, venison or turkey.

- Now cook ground beef until completely tendered.

- Use boiling water to rinse the fat off the beef by putting it into a colander covered with cheesecloth. You may need to do this process a few times to make sure that you have removed the fat. Preheat the dehydrator to 160-170° for 35 minutes. Take your ground beef and place it on dehydrator trays. Using fruit leather sheets is the easiest way to prevent any particles from escaping the dehydrator trays.

- Dehydrate the ground beef until it is completely dried. It will look similar to a small pebble. Depending on the dehydrator this process could take between 7-12 hours the moisture within your home can also effect the process time.

- After that process is complete allow the meat to cool.

- Place the meat into a sterilized mason jars, fill up to 2 inches from the top of jar.

- Add oxygen absorbers to your filled jars and tighten the lids.

- Store the canning jars in an area such as a cold cellar that is a nice dark and cool place.

The Secret to Dehydrating Chicken

Ingredients and directions on how to make chicken. Place the chicken breasts in the brine or oil-free marinate for one to two days. The brine recipe I shared is enough for 6 midsized chicken breasts.

Brine for Chicken Ingredients:

Mix the following ingredients then boil in pot and mix it well to make sure that the sugar and salt are well blended and dissolved.

- 3 teaspoons of salt

- 2 litres of water

- 4 teaspoons of sugar

- 1 bay leaf

- 2 cloves

- 1/2 tablespoon of peppercorns

Directions:

When the liquid has cooled down, place it into fridge and wait for it to get really nice and chilled before you add in the chicken breasts. Cover the chicken completely with the brine. Leave in the fridge for two days. Cook chicken breasts in pressure cooker for 12 minutes or until done.

Cook for about 20 minutes. Add a cup of water to the pressure cooker then allow to cool. Cut the chicken into small slices. The thinner the slices of chicken are the quicker you can dehydrate them. Chicken breasts seem to be the easiest parts to cut nice and thin to dehydrate. Next you need to dehydrate the chicken in an oven or dehydrator. If you use your oven do not shut oven door completely.

The temperature should be 122°F, I set my temperature of my food dehydrator a little higher. Keep dehydrating chicken until it completely dries. It can take 8-12 hours depending on the size of the chicken pieces and the oven. You will know when it is done when the chicken has darkened and breaks easily. Store in a cool and dry place.

When you are prepping, hydrate the chicken by soaking it in water for at least an hour before you begin cooking. You can boil the chicken in liquid such as soup to make it soft.

Salmon Jerky

- Ingredients for Brine:
- 1 teaspoon of lemon juice
- 1 cup of water
- 1 half tablespoon of sea salt
- half a teaspoon of garlic powder

- half a teaspoon of onion powder

- 1 teaspoon of paprika

- half a cup of cider vinegar

Directions:

Freeze your clean piece of salmon for at least 30 minutes or until it is firm. This will help make it easier to cut. Remove the flesh from the salmon and cut into pieces. Mix the ingredients for your brine in a bowl. Add in the salmon pieces and allow them to soak for 12 hours in the fridge.

Take out from fridge and lay salmon pieces on paper towel. Place the salmon pieces onto the dehydrator tray. Dehydrate salmon for 3-4 hours at 145° Fahrenheit. It will turn a dark reddish color when it is done. It should be dry and chewy. Store the salmon in a ball jar for many months. Enjoy the great health benefits of salmon anywhere, no matter what season you are in.

Salmon Jerky Nutrition

There are many health benefits connected to salmon. Here is a list of some of those healthy perks:

high amounts of omega 3 (this will help blood flow and brain functioning)

Vitamin D

high in protein

selenium (helps to fight stress and supports thyroid)

B12 (helps in supporting good nerve functioning)

Vegetable Dehydrator Recipes

Eggplant Bacon

Ingredients:

- 2 teaspoons of maple syrup

- 2 teaspoons of olive oil

- 1 eggplant

- 2 teaspoons of cider vinegar

- 2 teaspoons of soy sauce

- 2 tablespoons of paprika

- half a tablespoon of salt

- pinch of black pepper

Directions:

In a small bowl mix all the ingredients except for the eggplant. Peel and slice the eggplant into thin layers. Add eggplant into bowl with sauce and leave there to marinate for a few minutes. Place eggplant onto mesh oven tray.

Dehydrator

Dehydrate at 115° -125° Fahrenheit for 24 hours.

Oven

Turn oven to 75° C and cook for an hour.

Chapter 3. Survival Meal Recipes

1. Chicken Soup

Ingredients:

- 1 cup of freeze-dried chicken

- 3 cups of egg noodles

- 3 tablespoons of chicken soup powder

- 1/4 cup of onion, dried, chopped

- 1/4 cup of celery, dried, chopped

- half a cup of carrots, dried, chopped

- half a cup of mushrooms, dried, sliced

- 1/4 tablespoon of black pepper

- 1/4 tablespoon of oregano, dried

- 1 tablespoon of parsley, dried, chopped

- 1 tablespoon of lemon juice

Directions:

Mix all the ingredients in a large bowl. Add the ingredients into a jar and top jar
with oxygen absorber and close tightly. When you are ready to prepare the soup
boil 6 cups of water and add in the soup jar contents. Simmer for 15 minutes
allow contents to soften.

2. Hungarian Goulash

Ingredients:

- 2 pounds of stewing beef
- 4 teaspoons of paprika
- 2 tablespoons of mustard powder
- 4 white onions, sliced
- 4 cloves of garlic
- 1 teaspoon of olive oil
- water as needed
- half a cup of vinegar
- 1 can of tomato puree
- 2 bell peppers
- 6 potatoes, chopped
- 4 carrots, sliced

Directions:

Mix paprika, salt and dry mustard in bowl. In large pot heat the olive oil and saute the garlic and onions. Dip the stewing meat in with the spice mixture then place into pot with onions and garlic and brown.

Layer the meat in mason jars along with mixed veggies of peppers, carrots, and potatoes. Add in 5 cups of water and vinegar and can of tomato paste and mix with seasonings. Boil then pore hot liquid over the layered meat and veggies. Use knife to get rid of any air pockets in jars.

3. Beef Stroganoff

Ingredients:

- 4 pounds of sliced beef
- 2 teaspoons of Worcestershire sauce
- 1 teaspoon of butter
- 4 cups of mushrooms, sliced
- 4 cloves of garlic, chopped
- 2 onions, sliced, chopped
- pepper and salt to taste
- water as needed

Directions:

In a large pot, fry beef, onions, garlic and mushrooms in butter until golden browned. Mix in Worcestershire sauce and water. Pour 1 cup of water and stir well until it boils. Put the Stroganoff into sterilized jars spreading the sauce evenly across jars. Cover the jars and process for half an hour at 10 pounds of pressure.

4. Sweet & Sour Chicken with Rice

Ingredients:

- 10 ounces of frozen chicken nuggets
- 1 large green pepper, cut into 1 inch pieces
- 1 eight ounce can of pineapple chunks
- 1 and a half cups of rice
- 1 can of sliced water chestnuts, drained
- half a tablespoon of instant chicken granules
- 2 tablespoons of soy sauce
- 2 tablespoons of cornstarch
- 3 tablespoons of sugar
- 1/4 cup of white vinegar

Directions:

Bake or fry chicken nuggets according to package directions. Boil the rice. Drain the pineapples, but save juice. Add in enough water to the saved juice to make 1 and a half cups of liquid. Pour pineapple juice mix into pan.

Add some sweet pepper and boil then reduce heat. Cover and cook for 2 minutes. Stir vinegar, cornstarch, sugar, soy sauce and bouillon granules. Add into pan. Cook over medium heat until thickened. Add in pineapple chunks and chicken and water chestnuts. Pour chicken mix over cooked rice.

5. Chicken Cacciatore

Ingredients:

- 1 kg of chicken, boneless, skinless, cut into small pieces
- 2 teaspoons of thyme
- 2 teaspoons of basil
- 2 teaspoons of oregano
- 1 bottle of vinegar
- 4 cups of tomatoes, chopped
- 4 cloves of garlic, chopped
- 2 cups of mushrooms, cubed
- 2 cups of onion, cubed
- 2 cups of peppers, cubed
- salt and pepper to taste

Directions:

Layer onions, chicken, mushroom, peppers, and garlic into mason jars. In a large stockpot bring the vinegar, tomatoes, and herbs to a boil. Pour the hot liquid over the layered ingredients in your jars. Cover the jars and submerge in hot water and boil for 10 minutes. Leave jars to rest overnight on counter top.

6. Simple Biscuits

Ingredients:

- 1 cup of flour

- 1/2 cup of buttermilk

- 1/4 cup of shortening

- 2 tablespoons of baking powder

- 1/4 tablespoon of salt

Directions:

Mix flour and baking powder with salt in a bowl. Cut in the shortening. Add in the milk and mix to make dough. Make small size biscuits. Place on baking sheet that is greased and bake at 400° Fahrenheit for 20 minutes.

7. Linguine with Artichokes & Leeks

Ingredients:

- one pound of linguine

- 2 cups of Parmesan cheese, freshly grated

- spices to taste

- 2 tablespoons of lemon juice

- 12-ounce jar of marinated artichoke hearts in oil, halved, and drained

- 3 medium leeks, divide lengthwise and cut into 1-inch pieces

- 2 tablespoons of olive oil

Directions:

Boil the pasta according to package directions, save half a cup of the cooking water. Put pasta into large bowl. Heat oil over medium flame, remove leeks and put aside. Place artichokes into pan and cook for 4 minutes per side. Put leeks back into skillet and saute with artichokes.

Add in lemon juice, salt and pepper. Put veggies in pasta and saute with half of the Parmesan cheese. Add in some of saved cooking water if needed. Sprinkle the remaining cheese on top.

8. Linguine Marvini

Ingredients:

- 1 pound of thin linguine
- few fresh basil leaves
- 6 tablespoons of Parmesan cheese, fresh, grated
- 2 tablespoons of fresh ground pepper
- 2 tablespoons of salt
- 1 cup of butter
- 3 cloves of garlic, thinly sliced
- 2 tablespoons of olive oil

Directions:

Boil the pasta according to the package instructions. Heat oil in pan over medium heat adding in garlic for about 2 minutes. Reduce heat to low and put in butter, lemon juice, salt and pepper and 4 tablespoons of Parmesan cheese. Turn of the heat. Add in the basil and mix. Add remaining cheese on top.

9. Lasagna-Style Baked Ziti

Ingredients:

- 1 ounce of ziti
- 2-ounces of marinara sauce
- spices to taste
- 1 pound of beef
- 4 cloves of garlic, finely chopped
- 3 large white onions, finely chopped
- 2 tablespoons of olive oil
- 1 bunch of spinach, thick stems removed
- 1 cup of ricotta cheese
- 2 cups of Parmesan cheese, grated
- 4 cups of Mozzarella cheese, grated

Directions:

Preheat oven to 400° Fahrenheit. Boil pasta according to package directions. Drain it and put aside. Heat the oil in pan in medium heat. Add in garlic and onion and saute for 5 minutes.

Add in the beef, spices and stir for about six minutes cook. Add in pasta with meat mix and blend in well. Add marinara sauce, spinach, and 1/4 cup of Parmesan cheese. Transfer to baking dish. Sprinkle with mozzarella and top with remaining Parmesan cheese. Bake until cheese is totally melted.

10. Hot Italian Sausage & Tomato Pasta

Ingredients:

- 1 pound of dry fettucine

- 1 cup of Parmesan cheese

- 1 cup of arugula, chopped

- 1 cup of basil leaves, fresh chopped

- 2 teaspoons of black pepper

- 2 teaspoons of salt

- 7 tablespoons of white vinegar

- 6 pints of red cherry tomatoes

- 5 hot sausages, casings removed

- 4 cloves of garlic, minced

- 3 white onions, sliced

- 2 tablespoons of olive oil

Directions:

Boil the fettucine according to the package directions. Drain and put aside. Heat oil over medium heat. Add in onion and minced garlic. Cook for 2 minutes. Add in sausage and cook for additional five minutes.

Add in tomatoes and cook for 10 minutes. Put in vinegar, and spices. Add in the boiled fettucine, arugula and basil, mix. Serve in bowls and sprinkle with Parmesan cheese.

11. Broccoli Spaghetti

Ingredients:

- 1 packet of spaghetti

- 1 tablespoon of red pepper flakes

- pepper to taste

- 1 rotisserie chicken, meat shredded, two cups

- 1 teaspoon of salt

- 4 garlic cloves, thinly sliced

- 1 cup of olive oil

- 1 large head of broccoli

Directions:

Take spaghetti and boil it in water with a pinch of salt and tablespoon of oil. Drain it out. Cut broccoli into small pieces. Heat half of the oil over medium heat, add in the broccoli, 1/4 teaspoon of salt and garlic.

Cook for 5 minutes. Add in pasta, saved pasta water, chicken more salt and pepper. Cook until it is heated evenly for about five minutes. Sprinkle the crushed red pepper and toss well. Drizzle remaining oil before serving.

12. Herbal Potatoes

Ingredients:

- 3 large potatoes
- garlic salt
- 2 tablespoons of oil
- 1/2 tablespoon of rosemary
- 1/2 tablespoon of sage
- 1/2 tablespoon of thyme
- 1/2 tablespoon of oregano
- 1/2 tablespoon of pepper, fresh ground

Directions:

Preheat your oven to 325° Fahrenheit. Cut potatoes into 1/4 inch slices. Place potatoes on greased oven trays. Mix pepper, oregano, sage, rosemary, and thyme in bowl. Brush the potatoes with oil and sprinkle herb mix onto them. Bake for 20 minutes.

13. Pepsi Chicken

Ingredients:

- 4 chicken breasts, skinless, boneless, hammered to 1/4 inch of thickness

- 1 teaspoon of honey

- 1/4 cup of barbecue sauce

- 1/2 cup of tomato ketchup

- 1 can of Pepsi

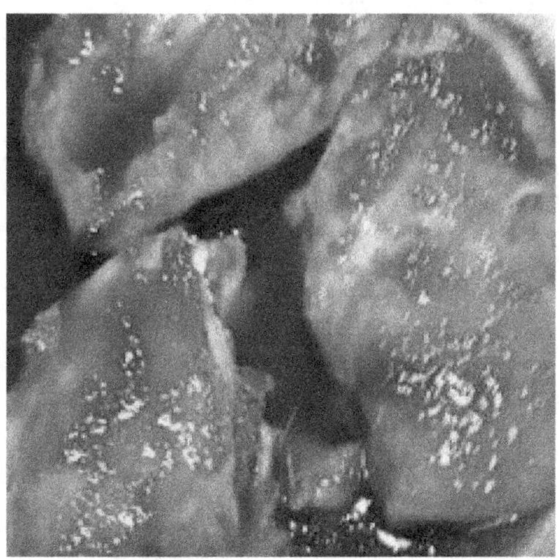

Directions:

Put all of the ingredients into into a pan and boil them. Cover and cook for 20 minutes. Remove the cover and cook for an additional 10 minutes.

14. Shrimps with Pasta

Ingredients:

- 1 pound of shrimp, deveined, peeled, raw
- half a teaspoon of lemon zest
- pepper and salt to taste
- 2 leeks, halved lengthwise then crosswise
- 2 tablespoons of butter
- 3/4 pound of gemelli, fusilli or any pasta you like

Directions:

Boil the pasts in water along with some salt and oil. Heat the butter in pan over medium heat. Add in all the ingredients and mix well. Cook until hot.

15. *Chicken & Dumplings*

Ingredients:

- 1 packet of biscuits

- two stalks of celery, chopped

- 1 pound of chicken breast, skinless, boneless, cut into bite-size pieces

- salt and pepper

Directions:

Cook the chicken either in a pan or pot. Once chicken is cooked add it into a pot of boiling water. Add in the celery. Drop biscuits into pot in bite-size pieces. Let boil and serve.

16. Survival Chinese

Ingredients:

- 1 pound of hamburger meat

- 2 packages of Ramen

- 1 package or can of mixed veggies

Directions:

Cook the burger on stove over medium heat until done. In a separate dish, cook the ramen noodles. Once they are done add in the season packet and drain most of liquid off. Add in the veggies and mix all and serve.

17. Lumberjack Salad

Ingredients:

- 1/4 of a cup of raisins

- half a cup of nuts of your choice

- leaves for salad of your choice

Directions:

If you are looking for edibles you can use grass to make your salad, shorter grass is easier to digest. Dandelions and chickweed are also edible. You can use dandelion leaves in your salad.

18. Peanut Butter Shake

Ingredients:

- 1 cup of powdered milk

- 1 tablespoon of flax, ground

- 2 tablespoons of Chia seeds

- 1/2 cup of powdered peanut butter

Directions:

Place the contents into a water bottle, fill halfway with water and shake well.

19. Peanut Butter Protein Bites

Ingredients:

- 1 cup of powdered milk
- 3 cups of oats
- 1/3 cup of chocolate chips
- 1 cup of peanut butter

Directions:

Combine all of the ingredients in a bowl and wrap each bite in a piece of foil. You can wrap multiple bites in foil for minimal space. These can last up to several days. If you are heading out to the woods you can pack at least a dozen.

20. Beans & Shrooms

Ingredients:

- 1 package of mushrooms, sliced
- 1 white onion, chopped
- pepper and salt to taste
- 2 cans of baked beans

Directions:

Open the cans of beans and place in pan over a fire. Add in the mushrooms and salt and pepper as well as the onion. Simmer for 10 minutes

21. *Easy Tomato Mac*

Ingredients:

- 1 package of macaroni
- 2 large tomatoes
- salt and pepper to taste
- 1 package of cheese sauce

Directions:

Fill a pot halfway with water and bring it to a boil. Add in macaroni and let it boil, slice and chop tomato. Mix all of the ingredients into pot with macaroni and mix well.

22. *Easy Flat Bread*

Ingredients:

- 1 teaspoon of baking soda
- water
- 1 cup of whole wheat flour

Directions:

Mix the ingredients in a bowl so it becomes like a dough. Wrap in foil and place near hot coals. You may need to let it bake for about half an hour. Let it stand for a few moments then enjoy!

23. *Field Hummus*

Ingredients:

- 1 tablespoon of sesame seeds

- 1 white onion, chopped

- 1 teaspoon of garlic powder

- 1 large can of chickpeas

Directions:

Mash the chickpeas in a pot and in sesame seeds followed by garlic and other spices. Add in onions and a bit of water. Heat over fire until hot.

24. *Fish Fry Over Open Fire*

Ingredients:

- Trout or whatever fish you catch

- 1 lemon

- salt and pepper to taste

- green beans

Directions:

Clean fish and place it inside piece of foil. Slice lemon and slide it into the fish and sprinkle with salt and pepper. Wrap the fish in foil. Set in the fire to cook for about 10 minutes. Add beans to a pot and heat over fire. Add some lemon juice to them and seasoning. Once all is heated up enjoy your meal cooked over the open fire!

25. Mini Tuna Pizza Bites

Ingredients:

- 1 package of saltine crackers
- 2 cans of tuna
- Mozzarella cheese
- 1 jar of tomato paste

Directions:

Open the jars and drain the tuna. On saltine crackers apply some tomato paste then tuna, and some cheese and enjoy!

Conclusion

I hope that you and your loved ones will enjoy trying out these easy to follow and prepare recipes they will sure come in handy during survival periods or when out in the woods hiking or just for something easy to whip up!

We do not like to think that we could end up in a situation where we are left to rely on emergency supply foods, but it is always better to be safe than sorry. I can assure you that you will feel more safe and secure in knowing that you do have some emergency supplies of foods at the ready just in case you find yourself and loved ones in an emergency situation. You will find some comfort in knowing that you have made some preparations for such times.

I wish to thank you once again for downloading my book, I appreciate your support of my work.   I would really love to read your input in a review on Amazon of my book, it would be most appreciated!